Rookie biographies®

Benjamin Franklin
Revised Edition

By Wil Mara

Reading Consultant
Cecilia Minden-Cupp, PhD
Former Director of the Language and Literacy Program
Harvard Graduate School of Education
Cambridge, Massachusetts

Children's Press®
A Division of Scholastic Inc.
New York Toronto London Auckland Sydney
Mexico City New Delhi Hong Kong
Danbury, Connecticut

Designer: Herman Adler Design
Photo Researcher: Caroline Anderson
The photo on the cover shows Benjamin Franklin.

Library of Congress Cataloging-in-Publication Data

Benjamin Franklin / by Wil Mara.— Rev. ed.
    p. cm. — (Rookie biography)
ISBN-10: 0-531-12450-9 (lib. bdg.)   0-531-12591-2 (pbk.)
ISBN-13: 978-0-531-12450-5 (lib. bdg.)   978-0-531-12591-5 (pbk.)
    1. Franklin, Benjamin, 1706–1790—Juvenile literature. 2. Statesmen—
United States— Biography—Juvenile literature. 3. Scientists—United States—
Biography—Juvenile literature. 4. Inventors—United States—Biography—
Juvenile literature. 5. Printers—United States—Biography—Juvenile literature.
I. Title. II. Series.
E302.6.F8M28 2007
973.3092—dc22
                                                        2006004645

CHILDREN'S PRESS, and ROOKIE BIOGRAPHIES®, and associated
logos are trademarks and/or registered trademarks of Scholastic Library
Publishing. SCHOLASTIC and associated logos are trademarks and/or
registered trademarks of Scholastic Inc.

1 2 3 4 5 6 7 8 9 10 R 16 15 14 13 12 11 10 09 08 07

Do you like to do different things? Benjamin Franklin did. He was an inventor, printer, author, and scientist. He also helped to make a new country.

4

Franklin was born just over 300 years ago, in Boston, Massachusetts. His birthdate is January 17, 1706.

When Ben was a young man, he helped his brother, James, run a newspaper. He printed the pages and made sure all the words were spelled correctly.

In 1726, he moved to

Philadelphia, Pennsylvania.

He started his own newspaper.

It was called the *Pennsylvania*

Gazette.

In 1730, Franklin married a woman named Deborah Read. They had two children—one boy and one girl.

Franklin liked to do science experiments. His most famous experiment was very dangerous. He flew a kite with a key on its string during a storm. The key became electrified. Franklin wanted to show that lightning is electricity.

Franklin was very good at inventing things. He invented the rocking chair.

He also invented special eyeglasses called bifocals. Bifocals help you to see things up close and far away, too.

Franklin helped create Philadelphia's first library and fire department. He also started a school called the University of Pennsylvania.

In the mid 1700s, the people of America did not live in states. They lived in areas called colonies (KAWL-uh-neez) under the control of another country—England. They had to follow rules made by King George III.

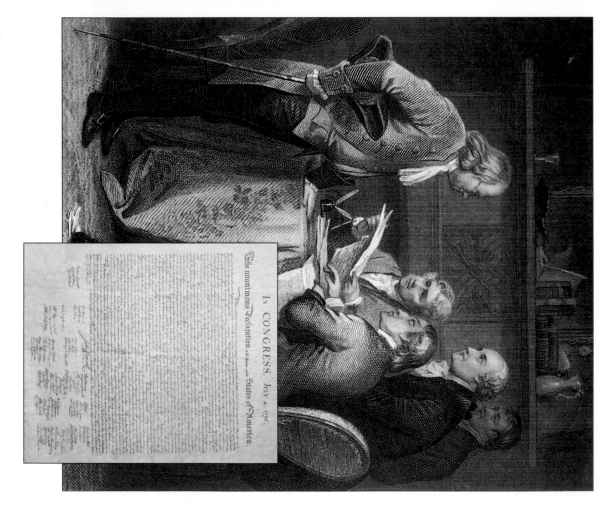

The people of America did not like living under England's control. Franklin helped write the Declaration (dek-luh-RAY-shun) of Independence (in-di-PEN-duhnss).

This important document told King George III that the colonists wanted to make their own rules.

The colonists fought a war with England to win their freedom. This was called the Revolutionary (rev-uh-LOO-shun-air-ee) War.

The colonists won the war in 1781. They named their new country the United States of America. Franklin helped make new laws and rules. These were written down in another famous document—the Constitution.

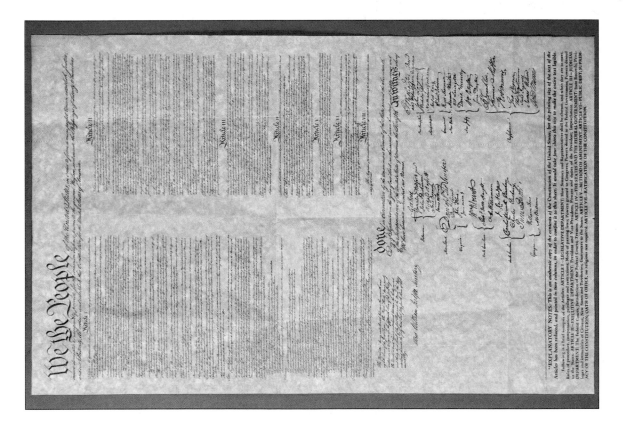

Franklin made many improvements to the postal system before and after the Revolutionary War. He wanted mail service to be faster and more reliable.

In 1775, he became the first Postmaster General of the United States.

Benjamin Franklin died on April 17, 1790, at the age of 84.

He made life better for the people of America. Many of his ideas and inventions are still part of our everyday lives.

Words You Know

Declaration of
Independence

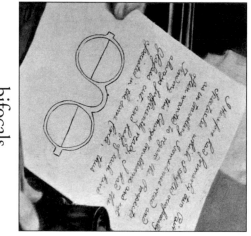

bifocals

electricity

Constitution

printer

University of Pennsylvania

Benjamin Franklin

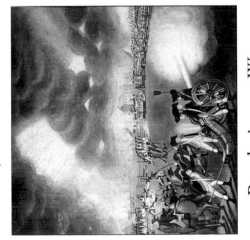

Revolutionary War

Index

About the Author

Wil Mara has authored more than seventy books, both fiction and nonfiction, for children and adults.

Photo Credits

Photographs © 2007: American Philosophical Society Library, Philadelphia: 11; Bridgeman Art Library International Ltd., London/New York: 7, 31 top right (New York Historical Society); Corbis Images: 3, 8, 15, 16, 19, 30 top left, 31 top left, 31 bottom right (Bettmann), 28 (Richard Cummins); Getty Images: 4 (Archive Photo), 23, 31 bottom left (Hulton|Archive); Library of Congress: cover; National Postal Museum, Smithsonian Institution, Washington, DC: 27; North Wind Picture Archives: 24; Stock Montage, Inc.: 12, 20, 30 bottom right; Superstock, Inc.: 20 inset, 25, 30 top right, 30 bottom left.